MAD LIBS®

GHOST STORY MAD LIBS

by Captain Foolhardy

MAD LIBS
An imprint of Penguin Random House LLC, New York

First published in the United States of America by Mad Libs,
an imprint of Penguin Random House LLC, New York, 2023

Mad Libs format and text copyright © 2023 by Penguin Random House LLC

Concept created by Roger Price & Leonard Stern

Cover illustration by Scott Brooks

Visit us online at penguinrandomhouse.com.

Printed in the United States of America

ISBN 9780593658376
5 7 9 10 8 6
COMR

MAD LIBS®

INSTRUCTIONS

MAD LIBS® is a game for people who don't like games!
It can be played by one, two, three, four, or forty.

● RIDICULOUSLY SIMPLE DIRECTIONS

In this tablet you will find stories containing blank spaces where words
are left out. One player, the READER, selects one of these stories. The
READER does not tell anyone what the story is about. Instead, he/she asks
the other players, the WRITERS, to give him/her words. These words are
used to fill in the blank spaces in the story.

● TO PLAY

The READER asks each WRITER in turn to call out a word—an adjective or
a noun or whatever the space calls for—and uses them to fill in the blank
spaces in the story. The result is a MAD LIBS® game.

When the READER then reads the completed MAD LIBS® game to the other
players, they will discover that they have written a story that is fantastic,
screamingly funny, shocking, silly, crazy, or just plain dumb—depending
upon which words each WRITER called out.

● EXAMPLE (*Before* and *After*)

"_____!" he said _____
　　　　　EXCLAMATION　　　　　　　　　　　　　　ADVERB

as he jumped into his convertible _____ and
　　　　　　　　　　　　　　　　　　　　　　NOUN

drove off with his _____ wife.
　　　　　　　　　　ADJECTIVE

"_____OUCH_____!" he said _____HAPPILY_____
　　　EXCLAMATION　　　　　　　　　　　ADVERB

as he jumped into his convertible _____CAT_____ and
　　　　　　　　　　　　　　　　　　　　NOUN

drove off with his _____BRAVE_____ wife.
　　　　　　　　　ADJECTIVE

In case you have forgotten what adjectives, adverbs, nouns, and verbs are, here is a quick review:

An ADJECTIVE describes something or somebody. *Lumpy, soft, ugly, messy,* and *short* are adjectives.

An ADVERB tells how something is done. It modifies a verb and usually ends in "ly." *Modestly, stupidly, greedily,* and *carefully* are adverbs.

A NOUN is the name of a person, place, or thing. *Sidewalk, umbrella, bridle, bathtub,* and *nose* are nouns.

A VERB is an action word. *Run, pitch, jump,* and *swim* are verbs. Put the verbs in past tense if the directions say PAST TENSE. *Ran, pitched, jumped,* and *swam* are verbs in the past tense.

When we ask for A PLACE, we mean any sort of place: a country or city (*Spain, Cleveland*) or a room (*bathroom, kitchen*).

An EXCLAMATION or SILLY WORD is any sort of funny sound, gasp, grunt, or outcry, like *Wow!, Ouch!, Whomp!, Ick!,* and *Gadzooks!*

When we ask for specific words, like a NUMBER, a COLOR, an ANIMAL, or a PART OF THE BODY, we mean a word that is one of those things, like *seven, blue, horse,* or *head.*

When we ask for a PLURAL, it means more than one. For example, *cat* pluralized is *cats.*

MAD LIBS® is fun to play with friends, but you can also play it by yourself! To begin with, DO NOT look at the story on the page below. Fill in the blanks on this page with the words called for. Then, using the words you have selected, fill in the blank spaces in the story.

Now you've created your own hilarious MAD LIBS® game!

TAKE THE LONG
WAY HOME

ADJECTIVE _____

PERSON YOU KNOW _____

ADJECTIVE _____

COLOR _____

ANIMAL _____

NOUN _____

CELEBRITY _____

VERB (PAST TENSE) _____

NOUN _____

VERB _____

NOUN _____

NUMBER _____

A PLACE _____

VERB _____

SAME CELEBRITY _____

VERB (PAST TENSE) _____

SAME PERSON YOU KNOW _____

NOUN _____

MAD⦾LIBS®
TAKE THE LONG WAY HOME

One dark and _____ night, a student named _____
        ADJECTIVE   PERSON YOU KNOW

decided to take a/an _____-cut through the _____
                          ADJECTIVE   COLOR

_____ Cemetery. But as soon as the student entered the creepy
     ANIMAL

_____-yard, a ghost appeared. It was a ghost named _____,
   NOUN   CELEBRITY

who _____ in a horrible _____ over two hundred
        VERB (PAST TENSE)   NOUN

years ago. "Who dares to _____ my eternal slumber?"
                                   VERB

demanded the ghost. The student hid behind a tombstone that was

shaped like a huge _____. They waited to say the
                              NOUN

ghost's name backward _____ times, so they could send
                              NUMBER

it back to the _____ it came from. When the ghost
                        A PLACE

was just about to _____ its victim, the student said,
                          VERB

"_____" backward three times! Then, the ghost
       SAME CELEBRITY

_____ into the ground and was never heard from again.
  VERB (PAST TENSE)

That was also the last time _____ tried to take a
                                    SAME PERSON YOU KNOW

short-_____ home.
        NOUN

From GHOST STORY MAD LIBS® • Copyright © 2023 by Penguin Random House LLC

MAD LIBS® is fun to play with friends, but you can also play it by yourself! To begin with, DO NOT look at the story on the page below. Fill in the blanks on this page with the words called for. Then, using the words you have selected, fill in the blank spaces in the story.

Now you've created your own hilarious MAD LIBS® game!

LETTER TO A GHOST

FIRST NAME _____

VERB ENDING IN "ING" _____

NOUN _____

VERB _____

A PLACE _____

NOUN _____

NUMBER _____

NOUN _____

ADVERB _____

ADJECTIVE _____

VERB _____

SOMETHING ALIVE _____

PLURAL NOUN _____

NOUN _____

ADJECTIVE _____

ADJECTIVE _____

ADVERB _____

YOUR NAME _____

MAD LIBS®

LETTER TO A GHOST

Dear _____ Phantasmic,
　　　　　　FIRST NAME

Hi! Hope you are floating well and _____ your
　　　　　　　　　　　　　　　　　VERB ENDING IN "ING"

after-_____! I wanted to _____ this letter to say
　　　　　NOUN　　　　　　　　　　　VERB

thank you for choosing to haunt my _____! Now I don't need
　　　　　　　　　　　　　　　　　A PLACE

to turn on the _____-conditioning during summer because
　　　　　　　　NOUN

your ghostly aura makes my room _____ degrees colder! Plus,
　　　　　　　　　　　　　　　　NUMBER

your creepy glow means I don't need a night-_____ to help
　　　　　　　　　　　　　　　　　　　　　　NOUN

me sleep. I also _____ like having someone to hang out with
　　　　　　　　　ADVERB

when I'm feeling _____ or when I feel like playing
　　　　　　　　　ADJECTIVE

_____-and-seek. And the best part of having a ghost is . . .
VERB

now my little _____ doesn't barge into my room to play
　　　　　　　SOMETHING ALIVE

with my collection of miniature _____! So, thanks for
　　　　　　　　　　　　　　　PLURAL NOUN

being such a great _____. Keep up the _____ work!
　　　　　　　　　NOUN　　　　　　　　　　　ADJECTIVE

I'm sure this is only the beginning of our _____ and boo-tiful
　　　　　　　　　　　　　　　　　　　ADJECTIVE

friendship!

_____ yours,
ADVERB

_____
YOUR NAME

MAD LIBS® is fun to play with friends, but you can also play it by yourself! To begin with, DO NOT look at the story on the page below. Fill in the blanks on this page with the words called for. Then, using the words you have selected, fill in the blank spaces in the story.

Now you've created your own hilarious MAD LIBS® game!

HOW TO GET RID OF GHOSTS

PLURAL NOUN _____

VERB _____

NUMBER _____

SILLY WORD _____

VERB ENDING IN "ING" _____

TYPE OF LIQUID _____

PLURAL NOUN _____

VERB _____

ARTICLE OF CLOTHING (PLURAL) _____

VERB _____

PART OF THE BODY _____

TYPE OF FOOD (PLURAL) _____

ADJECTIVE _____

A PLACE _____

VERB ENDING IN "ING" _____

ADVERB _____

VERB _____

ADJECTIVE _____

MAD LIBS
HOW TO GET RID OF GHOSTS

Follow these simple _____ to make sure your room is free

PLURAL NOUN

of ghosts! Ghosts love to _____ under the bed. To scare them

VERB

off, get on your bed and do _____ jumping jacks while screaming

NUMBER

"_____!" That will send those ghosts _____

SILLY WORD   VERB ENDING IN "ING"

out the door. Then, check your closet by sniffing the air for the scent

of ecto-_____. If you smell anything, your closet is

TYPE OF LIQUID

probably haunted by _____! To get rid of them, _____

PLURAL NOUN   VERB

your dirty _____ on a hanger. Ghosts don't

ARTICLE OF CLOTHING (PLURAL)

_____ smelly socks. If you still can't find your ghost, go to the

VERB

kitchen, open the fridge with your _____, and get a bowl

PART OF THE BODY

of _____ 'n' cream ice cream. It's every ghost's

TYPE OF FOOD (PLURAL)

_____ dessert! Set the bowl of ice cream in your _____

ADJECTIVE   A PLACE

and wait for the ghost to come out of its _____ spot.

VERB ENDING IN "ING"

When it does, _____ ask the ghost to leave. Most ghosts will

ADVERB

_____ away if you use _____ manners!

VERB   ADJECTIVE

MAD LIBS® is fun to play with friends, but you can also play it by yourself! To begin with, DO NOT look at the story on the page below. Fill in the blanks on this page with the words called for. Then, using the words you have selected, fill in the blank spaces in the story.

Now you've created your own hilarious MAD LIBS® game!

GHOSTS: TRUE OR FALSE?

ADJECTIVE _____

VERB _____

ADJECTIVE _____

PLURAL NOUN _____

EXCLAMATION _____

A SOUND _____

TYPE OF LIQUID _____

TYPE OF CONTAINER _____

ADJECTIVE _____

VERB _____

SOMETHING ALIVE (PLURAL) _____

TYPE OF EVENT _____

PART OF THE BODY _____

NOUN _____

TYPE OF FOOD (PLURAL) _____

NUMBER _____

PLURAL NOUN _____

MAD LIBS®

GHOSTS: TRUE OR FALSE?

There are a lot of misunderstandings about ghosts, and here at the

_____ Academy of Ghosts, we're ready to _____ the
　　ADJECTIVE　　　　　　　　　　　　　　　　　　　　　VERB

record straight. Take this True or _____ quiz to test your
　　　　　　　　　　　　　　　　　　ADJECTIVE

knowledge of ghost _____!
　　　　　　　　　PLURAL NOUN

1. Ghosts like to scare humans with noises like " _____!" or
　　　　　　　　　　　　　　　　　　　　　　　EXCLAMATION

　　" _____!"
　　　　A SOUND

2. Ghosts are afraid of _____, so you should keep a full
　　　　　　　　　　　TYPE OF LIQUID

　　_____ with you at all times.
　　TYPE OF CONTAINER

3. If you see a ghost, you should stay _____ and
　　　　　　　　　　　　　　　　　　ADJECTIVE

　　_____ away slowly!
　　　　VERB

4. Ghosts only haunt human children and their pet

　　_____.
　　SOMETHING ALIVE (PLURAL)

5. To be a ghost at your next Halloween _____, cut
　　　　　　　　　　　　　　　　　TYPE OF EVENT

　　_____-size holes in a fitted _____.
　　PART OF THE BODY　　　　　　　　　　NOUN

6. Ghosts digest _____ _____ times faster
　　　　　　　TYPE OF FOOD (PLURAL)　　NUMBER

　　than _____ do.
　　　PLURAL NOUN

Answer Key: T, T, F, T, F, F

MAD LIBS® is fun to play with friends, but you can also play it by yourself! To begin with, DO NOT look at the story on the page below. Fill in the blanks on this page with the words called for. Then, using the words you have selected, fill in the blank spaces in the story.

Now you've created your own hilarious MAD LIBS® game!

THE CURSE OF THE SCHOOL LUNCH LADY

YOUR NAME _____

TYPE OF FOOD _____

TYPE OF BUILDING _____

A SOUND _____

ANIMAL _____

PLURAL NOUN _____

ADJECTIVE _____

TYPE OF FOOD (PLURAL) _____

PLURAL NOUN _____

PART OF THE BODY _____

ARTICLE OF CLOTHING _____

TYPE OF FOOD _____

EXCLAMATION _____

PART OF THE BODY _____

NOUN _____

NOUN _____

PART OF THE BODY (PLURAL) _____

ADJECTIVE _____

MAD LIBS®
THE CURSE OF THE SCHOOL LUNCH LADY

I, _____, the ghost hunter extraordinaire, have solved the
  YOUR NAME

mystery of the disappearing _____! Late last night, I went
                              TYPE OF FOOD

hunting for ghosts in my local high _____. Once inside, I
                                     TYPE OF BUILDING

heard a loud _____ coming from the cafeteria! I hoped it was
             A SOUND

our school's pet _____ stealing _____ again. But
                 ANIMAL   PLURAL NOUN

instead, I found a ghostly lunch lady making a very _____
                                                    ADJECTIVE

snack in the room. _____ covered the walls, the floor,
                   TYPE OF FOOD (PLURAL)

and all the folding _____. I felt a lump in my
                    PLURAL NOUN

_____ as I walked closer to the messy ghost. She was dressed
PART OF THE BODY

in a white _____ and floated off the ground as she ate
           ARTICLE OF CLOTHING

all our _____ nuggets! I cried out, "_____," to
        TYPE OF FOOD   EXCLAMATION

make the ghost stop, but she just burped in my _____!
                                               PART OF THE BODY

Then, I felt a cold _____ waft over me. The ghost's _____
                    NOUN   NOUN

was so smelly, I went weak in the _____ and fell
                                  PART OF THE BODY (PLURAL)

asleep. When I woke up, the ghost was _____!
                                      ADJECTIVE

MAD LIBS® is fun to play with friends, but you can also play it by yourself! To begin with, DO NOT look at the story on the page below. Fill in the blanks on this page with the words called for. Then, using the words you have selected, fill in the blank spaces in the story.

Now you've created your own hilarious MAD LIBS® game!

WOULD YOU RATHER?

ADJECTIVE _____

VERB _____

TYPE OF FOOD _____

SILLY WORD _____

PERSON YOU KNOW _____

CELEBRITY _____

OCCUPATION _____

COUNTRY _____

VERB ENDING IN "ING" _____

NUMBER _____

TYPE OF BUILDING _____

TYPE OF CONTAINER _____

ANIMAL _____

SOMETHING ALIVE _____

PART OF THE BODY _____

PART OF THE BODY _____

MAD LIBS

WOULD YOU RATHER?

Being haunted is never _____, but some ghosts
                                ADJECTIVE
_____ in worse ways than others. How would you like to be
  VERB
haunted?

- Would you rather be haunted by a ghost that smells like

  _____ *or* a ghost that screams "_____"?
    TYPE OF FOOD   SILLY WORD

- Would you rather be haunted by a ghost named _____
                                            PERSON YOU KNOW

  or _____?
       CELEBRITY

- Would you rather be haunted by a ghost who was a/an _____
                                            OCCUPATION

  from _____ *or* a family of ghosts that never stops
            COUNTRY

  _____?
  VERB ENDING IN "ING"

- Would you rather spend _____ years stuck in a haunted
                         NUMBER

  _____ *or* in a haunted _____?
  TYPE OF BUILDING   TYPE OF CONTAINER

- Would you rather be haunted by a ghost _____ *or* a ghost
                                        ANIMAL

  _____?
  SOMETHING ALIVE

- Would you rather be haunted by a terrifying ghost with a giant

  _____ *or* a hairy _____?
  PART OF THE BODY   PART OF THE BODY

MAD LIBS® is fun to play with friends, but you can also play it by yourself! To begin with, DO NOT look at the story on the page below. Fill in the blanks on this page with the words called for. Then, using the words you have selected, fill in the blank spaces in the story.

Now you've created your own hilarious MAD LIBS® game!

A HAUNTED SLUMBER PARTY

YOUR NAME _____

TYPE OF BUILDING _____

TYPE OF EVENT _____

ARTICLE OF CLOTHING (PLURAL) _____

PLURAL NOUN _____

VERB _____

OCCUPATION (PLURAL) _____

A PLACE _____

TYPE OF FOOD _____

SOMETHING ALIVE (PLURAL) _____

VERB _____

PART OF THE BODY (PLURAL) _____

ANIMAL _____

SILLY WORD _____

VERB _____

NOUN _____

ADJECTIVE _____

VERB ENDING IN "ING" _____

MAD LIBS
A HAUNTED
SLUMBER PARTY

Hi, my name is _____, and I live in a haunted
<u>YOUR NAME</u>

_____! Tonight, I'm having a/an _____
<u>TYPE OF BUILDING</u>   <u>TYPE OF EVENT</u>

with a bunch of ghosts! First, we'll build a fort out of pillows,

_____, and leftover _____. Then
<u>ARTICLE OF CLOTHING (PLURAL)</u>   <u>PLURAL NOUN</u>

we'll _____ inside the fort and pretend to be _____
<u>VERB</u>   <u>OCCUPATION (PLURAL)</u>

working in (the) _____! Once we're hungry, we'll order some
<u>A PLACE</u>

_____ pizza with extra _____ on top.
<u>TYPE OF FOOD</u>   <u>SOMETHING ALIVE (PLURAL)</u>

Ghosts love to _____ food, even though it passes right
<u>VERB</u>

through their _____! Then we'll watch scary movies
<u>PART OF THE BODY (PLURAL)</u>

like _____-*bumps* and Scooby _____. I hope the
<u>ANIMAL</u>   <u>SILLY WORD</u>

ghosts like my picks. They don't _____ easily but are tough
<u>VERB</u>

critics of scary movies. And the best _____ is, I'll fall asleep
<u>NOUN</u>

_____ and sound, knowing that my phantom friends are
<u>ADJECTIVE</u>

_____ over me.
<u>VERB ENDING IN "ING"</u>

MAD LIBS® is fun to play with friends, but you can also play it by yourself! To begin with, DO NOT look at the story on the page below. Fill in the blanks on this page with the words called for. Then, using the words you have selected, fill in the blank spaces in the story.

Now you've created your own hilarious MAD LIBS® game!

THE POSSESSED BIKE

A PLACE _____

NOUN _____

ADJECTIVE _____

PART OF THE BODY (PLURAL) _____

ADJECTIVE _____

VERB ENDING IN "ING" _____

ADVERB _____

PART OF THE BODY _____

VERB _____

ADVERB _____

VEHICLE _____

NUMBER _____

PLURAL NOUN _____

VERB ENDING IN "ING" _____

TYPE OF BUILDING _____

A SOUND _____

VERB ENDING IN "ING" _____

MAD☉LIBS®

THE POSSESSED BIKE

I was walking home from (the) _____, minding my own
A PLACE

_____. But something just didn't feel _____! I felt
NOUN ADJECTIVE

like two invisible _____ were staring at me the
PART OF THE BODY (PLURAL)

whole time. I finally turned around and saw . . . a/an _____
ADJECTIVE

bike riding behind me. But there was no one _____
VERB ENDING IN "ING"

it! The bike _____ rolled toward me and nudged my
ADVERB

_____ like it was trying to tell me something. *Since*
PART OF THE BODY

when do bikes _____ *on their own?* I thought to myself.
VERB

I needed to get home _____, so I decided to jump on the
ADVERB

_____. Suddenly, the bike sped ahead at _____ miles
VEHICLE NUMBER

per hour! And just when I thought _____ couldn't get any
PLURAL NOUN

weirder, the bike started _____ into the sky! Finally, the
VERB ENDING IN "ING"

bike landed in front of my _____. I hopped off the seat,
TYPE OF BUILDING

and the bell on the bike made a/an _____! I think it was the
A SOUND

possessed bike's way of _____ goodbye.
VERB ENDING IN "ING"

MAD LIBS® is fun to play with friends, but you can also play it by yourself! To begin with, DO NOT look at the story on the page below. Fill in the blanks on this page with the words called for. Then, using the words you have selected, fill in the blank spaces in the story.

Now you've created your own hilarious MAD LIBS® game!

AN INTERVIEW WITH BLOODY MARY

NUMBER _____

VERB _____

NOUN _____

ADJECTIVE _____

VERB ENDING IN "ING" _____

NOUN _____

NOUN _____

TYPE OF FOOD _____

PART OF THE BODY _____

SOMETHING ALIVE (PLURAL) _____

EXCLAMATION _____

ADJECTIVE _____

VERB _____

NOUN _____

ADJECTIVE _____

OCCUPATION _____

VERB _____

ADJECTIVE _____

MAD LIBS®
AN INTERVIEW WITH BLOODY MARY

Everyone knows if you say "Bloody Mary" _____ times in the
NUMBER

mirror, her ghost will _____. Find out about this famous
VERB

ghost's _____ in this exclusive interview!
NOUN

Eerie Ed: Hi, _____ Mary. Thanks for _____
ADJECTIVE   VERB ENDING IN "ING"

with us on the show today.

Bloody Mary: Oh, it's no _____, Ed.
NOUN

Eerie Ed: So, what's the real _____ behind Bloody Mary?
NOUN

Bloody Mary: Well, I slipped on a piece of _____
TYPE OF FOOD

and fell _____-first into the mirror! Now I haunt
PART OF THE BODY

_____ for fun.
SOMETHING ALIVE (PLURAL)

Eerie Ed: _____! That's a pretty _____ way
EXCLAMATION   ADJECTIVE

to _____.
VERB

Bloody Mary: Tell me about it. Being an evil _____ has
NOUN

given me such a/an _____ afterlife. It was much easier than
ADJECTIVE

being a wicked _____!
OCCUPATION

Eerie Ed: But why do you like to _____ people?
VERB

Bloody Mary: Because it's _____, duh!
ADJECTIVE

MAD LIBS® is fun to play with friends, but you can also play it by yourself! To begin with, DO NOT look at the story on the page below. Fill in the blanks on this page with the words called for. Then, using the words you have selected, fill in the blank spaces in the story.

Now you've created your own hilarious MAD LIBS® game!

DANGER: SPACE GHOSTS

NUMBER _____

ADJECTIVE _____

YOUR NAME _____

VERB ENDING IN "ING" _____

A SOUND _____

COLOR _____

PART OF THE BODY (PLURAL) _____

PLURAL NOUN _____

PART OF THE BODY (PLURAL) _____

VERB ENDING IN "ING" _____

SILLY WORD _____

VERB _____

ADJECTIVE _____

ARTICLE OF CLOTHING _____

VERB ENDING IN "ING" _____

SAME SILLY WORD _____

SOMETHING ALIVE (PLURAL) _____

TYPE OF EVENT _____

MAD LIBS

DANGER: SPACE GHOSTS

Spacedate _____.656-2. The inter-_____ spaceship
　　　　　　　NUMBER　　　　　　　　　　　　ADJECTIVE

named _____ 3000 was _____ through
　　　　YOUR NAME　　　　　　　VERB ENDING IN "ING"

deep space when the crew received a message that said: "Danger! Space

ghosts on board!" The spaceship's alarms made a loud _____,
　　　　　　　　　　　　　　　　　　　　　　　　　　A SOUND

and _____ warning lights flashed as space ghosts with tentacles
　　　COLOR

on their _____ appeared on the ship. The crew
　　　　PART OF THE BODY (PLURAL)

prepared to fight with their laser _____, but the ghosts
　　　　　　　　　　　　　　　PLURAL NOUN

yanked the weapons out of their _____! Then,
　　　　　　　　　　　PART OF THE BODY (PLURAL)

the ghosts started _____ in a circle around the crew,
　　　　　　VERB ENDING IN "ING"

singing, "Splurg-gurg! _____!" The crew was certain
　　　　　　　　　SILLY WORD

the ghosts were going to _____ _____ them for lunch! But
　　　　　　　　　　　VERB

fortunately, the _____ captain pulled a guitar out of her
　　　　　　ADJECTIVE

_____ and started _____ it! "SPLURG-
ARTICLE OF CLOTHING　　　　　VERB ENDING IN "ING"

GURG! _____!" she sang. It turned out the scary
　　　SAME SILLY WORD

space ghosts weren't there to attack the ship. They just wanted some

_____ to dance with! It was the best rock 'n' roll
SOMETHING ALIVE (PLURAL)

_____ that outer space had ever seen!
TYPE OF EVENT

MAD LIBS® is fun to play with friends, but you can also play it by yourself! To begin with, DO NOT look at the story on the page below. Fill in the blanks on this page with the words called for. Then, using the words you have selected, fill in the blank spaces in the story.

Now you've created your own hilarious MAD LIBS® game!

DO NOT ENTER

ADJECTIVE _____

A SOUND _____

NUMBER _____

OCCUPATION _____

VERB (PAST TENSE) _____

VEHICLE _____

PART OF THE BODY _____

VERB ENDING IN "ING" _____

TYPE OF BUILDING _____

SOMETHING ALIVE _____

YOUR NAME _____

YOUR NAME _____

VERB _____

VERB _____

PART OF THE BODY (PLURAL) _____

PERSON YOU KNOW _____

COLOR _____

TYPE OF FOOD _____

MAD LIBS

DO NOT ENTER

My friends warned me to never go near the _____ mansion
                                            ADJECTIVE
at the end of the street. They said people heard terrifying noises, like

"_____," coming from the creepy house, even though no one
    A SOUND
had been inside for over _____ years! According to legend, a
                            NUMBER
lonely fifth-grade _____ used to live there, back in 1856. But
                      OCCUPATION
I didn't believe the rumors. So, late one night, I _____
                                                      VERB (PAST TENSE)
out of my house and rode down the street on my ten-speed _____.
                                                            VEHICLE
My _____ was _____ as I opened
      PART OF THE BODY   VERB ENDING IN "ING"
the door to the haunted _____ and heard the ghost
                            TYPE OF BUILDING
of a/an _____ calling my name. "_____,
            SOMETHING ALIVE   YOUR NAME
_____! Will you _____ with me?" the voice asked.
    YOUR NAME   VERB
I turned to _____ out the door, but it was locked! Suddenly, I
                VERB
felt cold _____ grab my hands! I looked up
            PART OF THE BODY (PLURAL)
and saw . . . _____, the ghost with the glowing
                    PERSON YOU KNOW
_____ eyes! The stories were true, and I was about to become
    COLOR
dead _____!
        TYPE OF FOOD

MAD LIBS® is fun to play with friends, but you can also play it by yourself! To begin with, DO NOT look at the story on the page below. Fill in the blanks on this page with the words called for. Then, using the words you have selected, fill in the blank spaces in the story.

Now you've created your own hilarious MAD LIBS® game!

SONG TO SUMMON A GHOST!

PART OF THE BODY _____

SAME PART OF THE BODY _____

TYPE OF BUILDING _____

PLURAL NOUN _____

VERB _____

PERSON YOU KNOW _____

ADJECTIVE _____

SILLY WORD _____

ADJECTIVE _____

COLOR _____

VERB _____

ADJECTIVE _____

A SOUND _____

PLURAL NOUN _____

ADJECTIVE _____

PLURAL NOUN _____

MAD LIBS®
SONG TO SUMMON A GHOST!

Do you want to stand _____ to _____
PART OF THE BODY   SAME PART OF THE BODY

with a ghost? Then go into a haunted _____, turn off all the
TYPE OF BUILDING

_____, and sing this song . . .
PLURAL NOUN

Ghosty, ghosty, ghosty, we want to _____ you.
VERB

Come meet _____. Please say boo!
PERSON YOU KNOW

We're really _____—we don't bite.
ADJECTIVE

So come say _____. It'll be a fright!
SILLY WORD

People say you're _____, and we are, too!
ADJECTIVE

Are you red or _____? We hope you're blue.
COLOR

Can you _____ in the day, or only under moonlight?
VERB

We have so many _____ questions to ask all night!
ADJECTIVE

Ghosty, ghosty, ghosty, _____! That's your cue!
A SOUND

Make the _____ flicker out: Give us a clue!
PLURAL NOUN

Reveal your _____ form—no need to hide!
ADJECTIVE

We'll be best _____, even though you died!
PLURAL NOUN

MAD LIBS® is fun to play with friends, but you can also play it by yourself! To begin with, DO NOT look at the story on the page below. Fill in the blanks on this page with the words called for. Then, using the words you have selected, fill in the blank spaces in the story.

Now you've created your own hilarious MAD LIBS® game!

A HAUNTED CAMPING TRIP, PART 1

ADJECTIVE _____

SILLY WORD _____

TYPE OF LIQUID _____

ADJECTIVE _____

NOUN _____

PLURAL NOUN _____

TYPE OF FOOD _____

NOUN _____

PERSON YOU KNOW _____

VERB (PAST TENSE) _____

ADJECTIVE _____

EXCLAMATION _____

ARTICLE OF CLOTHING _____

SOMETHING ALIVE (PLURAL) _____

VERB _____

MAD LIBS®
A HAUNTED CAMPING TRIP, PART 1

At first, our camping trip was totally _____. My parents, best

ADJECTIVE

friend, and I played catch, swam in Lake _____'s crystal-clear

SILLY WORD

_____, and told _____ stories as we ate s'mores

TYPE OF LIQUID   ADJECTIVE

around the _____-fire. Then my parents went to sleep, and

NOUN

strange _____ started happening. First, the _____

PLURAL NOUN   TYPE OF FOOD

on my stick floated into the air and vanished! "That's the tastiest

_____ I've ever had!" said a mysterious voice. I thought it was

NOUN

just my friend, _____, messing with me. But then, my

PERSON YOU KNOW

friend's baseball cap _____ up into the air! We looked

VERB (PAST TENSE)

around in shock and saw . . . a/an _____ ghost behind us!

ADJECTIVE

"_____!" "If you want your baseball _____

EXCLAMATION   ARTICLE OF CLOTHING

back, follow me!" said the ghost. The ghost floated off into the dense

forest of _____ nearby. We were scared, but knew

SOMETHING ALIVE (PLURAL)

we had to _____ after my friend's favorite hat!

VERB

MAD LIBS® is fun to play with friends, but you can also play it by yourself! To begin with, DO NOT look at the story on the page below. Fill in the blanks on this page with the words called for. Then, using the words you have selected, fill in the blank spaces in the story.

Now you've created your own hilarious MAD LIBS® game!

A HAUNTED CAMPING TRIP, PART 2

ADJECTIVE _____

ARTICLE OF CLOTHING _____

VERB _____

PART OF THE BODY _____

VERB ENDING IN "ING" _____

NUMBER _____

A PLACE _____

ADJECTIVE _____

ARTICLE OF CLOTHING (PLURAL) _____

PLURAL NOUN _____

PLURAL NOUN _____

NOUN _____

CELEBRITY _____

FIRST NAME _____

NUMBER _____

ADJECTIVE _____

VERB _____

We chased the ghost into a field in the middle of the _____
ADJECTIVE

forest. "Give me back my _____!" screamed my BFF.
ARTICLE OF CLOTHING

Then I tried to _____ the ghost, but I flew right through
VERB

its _____! "Okay! Here you go!" said the ghost before
PART OF THE BODY

_____ the hat back to us. "You're just in time for Game
VERB ENDING IN "ING"

_____ of the Ghost _____ Series!" Suddenly, lots of
NUMBER   A PLACE

_____ ghosts appeared! They were all wearing matching
ADJECTIVE

baseball _____! Some had gloves made of
ARTICLE OF CLOTHING (PLURAL)

_____, and others carried wooden _____! A
PLURAL NOUN   PLURAL NOUN

huge crowd of ghosts descended from the _____-tops. Even
NOUN

the ghost of _____ was there to watch! Then, we realized
CELEBRITY

who everyone came to see: It was the ghost of Babe _____!
FIRST NAME

He hit the first pitch so hard, it flew _____ feet away! That night,
NUMBER

I learned that while ghosts may be _____, they sure know
ADJECTIVE

how to _____ a baseball bat!
VERB

MAD LIBS® is fun to play with friends, but you can also play it by yourself! To begin with, DO NOT look at the story on the page below. Fill in the blanks on this page with the words called for. Then, using the words you have selected, fill in the blank spaces in the story.

Now you've created your own hilarious MAD LIBS® game!

A SCARY TEST

ADJECTIVE _____

NUMBER _____

ADJECTIVE _____

PERSON YOU KNOW _____

A PLACE _____

NOUN _____

NOUN _____

VERB (PAST TENSE) _____

SILLY WORD _____

EXCLAMATION _____

PART OF THE BODY (PLURAL) _____

VERB (PAST TENSE) _____

NUMBER _____

TYPE OF LIQUID _____

ADJECTIVE _____

LAST NAME _____

NUMBER _____

LETTER OF THE ALPHABET _____

MAD LIBS

A SCARY TEST

Studying to be a ghost can be so _____! After _____

ADJECTIVE NUMBER

years of training at the _____ Academy of Ghosts, my teacher

ADJECTIVE

told me I had to scare my friend, _____, if I wanted to

PERSON YOU KNOW

graduate! When I arrived at my friend's _____, I found them

A PLACE

snuggled in a comfy _____, quietly reading their favorite

NOUN

scary _____. I carefully _____ behind them,

NOUN VERB (PAST TENSE)

took a deep breath, and yelled: "_____!" My friend screamed,

SILLY WORD

"_____," at the top of their _____ and

EXCLAMATION PART OF THE BODY (PLURAL)

_____ _____ feet out of their chair! They even

VERB (PAST TENSE) NUMBER

spilled iced _____ all over themselves! They were so

TYPE OF LIQUID

_____! It's safe to say my teacher, Mrs. Ghouley Von

ADJECTIVE

_____, taught me a thing or _____ about this

LAST NAME NUMBER

ghosting stuff. And the best part is, I got a/an _____+

LETTER OF THE ALPHABET

on my final exam in ghost class!

MAD LIBS® is fun to play with friends, but you can also play it by yourself! To begin with, DO NOT look at the story on the page below. Fill in the blanks on this page with the words called for. Then, using the words you have selected, fill in the blank spaces in the story.

Now you've created your own hilarious MAD LIBS® game!

IS YOUR BFF A GHOST?

NOUN _____

PERSON YOU KNOW _____

A SOUND _____

PART OF THE BODY _____

VERB _____

TYPE OF BUILDING _____

COUNTRY _____

VERB _____

ADJECTIVE _____

PLURAL NOUN _____

ANIMAL (PLURAL) _____

COLOR _____

ARTICLE OF CLOTHING _____

TYPE OF FOOD _____

TYPE OF LIQUID _____

NUMBER _____

ADJECTIVE _____

MAD LIBS®

IS YOUR BFF A GHOST?

Answer these questions to find out if your best _____ is really a
                                                        NOUN
ghost:

- Does _____ make scary noises like "_____"?
         PERSON YOU KNOW   A SOUND
- Is their _____ cold when you _____ hands?
           PART OF THE BODY   VERB
- Do they invite you to creepy sleepovers at an abandoned

  _____ in _____?
  TYPE OF BUILDING   COUNTRY
- Can they _____ through walls?
             VERB
- Do they like to play _____ pranks on innocent
                           ADJECTIVE

  _____?
  PLURAL NOUN
- Are your pet _____ afraid of them?
               ANIMAL (PLURAL)
- Do they wear the same _____ _____
                            COLOR   ARTICLE OF CLOTHING

  every day?

- Does their room smell like rotten _____?
                                     TYPE OF FOOD
- When they drink _____, does it pass right through
                   TYPE OF LIQUID

  them?

If you answered yes to _____ or more of these questions, your
                        NUMBER
BFF might be a/an _____ ghost!
                   ADJECTIVE

MAD LIBS® is fun to play with friends, but you can also play it by yourself! To begin with, DO NOT look at the story on the page below. Fill in the blanks on this page with the words called for. Then, using the words you have selected, fill in the blank spaces in the story.

Now you've created your own hilarious MAD LIBS® game!

ZOO BOO

NOUN _____

ANIMAL _____

ADVERB _____

VERB ENDING IN "ING" _____

ANIMAL (PLURAL) _____

TYPE OF BUILDING _____

ADJECTIVE _____

PART OF THE BODY _____

NUMBER _____

A PLACE _____

TYPE OF LIQUID _____

OCCUPATION _____

VERB _____

PLURAL NOUN _____

NOUN _____

VERB (PAST TENSE) _____

TYPE OF FOOD _____

OCCUPATION _____

MAD LIBS

ZOO BOO

The Metropolitan Zoo used to be the happiest on the _____.
NOUN

But after the ghost of a lion appeared in the _____ habitat,
ANIMAL

the zoo became _____ scary. The lion started by
ADVERB

_____ the feathers off the tropical _____
VERB ENDING IN "ING" ANIMAL (PLURAL)

in the _____. Then, it scared the zoo's _____
TYPE OF BUILDING ADJECTIVE

tortoise! After that night, the turtle didn't peek its _____
PART OF THE BODY

out of its shell for _____ whole weeks. Next, the lion started
NUMBER

haunting the _____-keepers as they were drinking _____
A PLACE TYPE OF LIQUID

in the break room! Finally, a ghost _____ was hired to
OCCUPATION

_____ the ghost. She set up lots of booby _____
VERB PLURAL NOUN

all over the zoo. She even had a special electromagnetic _____
NOUN

that she used to see ghosts in the dark! But no matter what she tried,

the lion always _____ through her fingers. That is, until
VERB (PAST TENSE)

she put some _____ out as bait! So much for the _____
TYPE OF FOOD OCCUPATION

of the jungle!

MAD LIBS® is fun to play with friends, but you can also play it by yourself! To begin with, DO NOT look at the story on the page below. Fill in the blanks on this page with the words called for. Then, using the words you have selected, fill in the blank spaces in the story.

Now you've created your own hilarious MAD LIBS® game!

DO YOU BELIEVE IN GHOSTS?

VERB _____

SOMETHING ALIVE (PLURAL) _____

PLURAL NOUN _____

NOUN _____

A PLACE _____

PART OF THE BODY (PLURAL) _____

VERB _____

CELEBRITY _____

FIRST NAME _____

ADJECTIVE _____

A SOUND _____

VERB ENDING IN "ING" _____

NOUN _____

PART OF THE BODY _____

NOUN _____

VERB _____

NOUN _____

PLURAL NOUN _____

MAD LIBS®
DO YOU BELIEVE IN GHOSTS?

Madame Gizelle here! _____ closer, my young
                              VERB

_____. Ghosts are nothing to be afraid of. In fact,
SOMETHING ALIVE (PLURAL)

there are many _____ floating around us right now! Don't
                   PLURAL NOUN

believe me? Then let me use my crystal _____ to summon one
                                             NOUN

of them to this small _____. First, close your
                            A PLACE

_____ and concentrate. Think of any person from
PART OF THE BODY (PLURAL)

history that you'd like to _____, like _____ or
                               VERB   CELEBRITY

_____ Washington! Then, repeat after me, "Ghost from the
FIRST NAME

_____ beyond, hear our call and then respond." Hear that
ADJECTIVE

_____? That bell tells us a ghost is _____ nearby.
A SOUND   VERB ENDING IN "ING"

Feel that cold _____ running up and down your
                      NOUN

_____? That is the _____ sitting next to you! And
PART OF THE BODY   NOUN

now, _____ your eyes and see for yourself! A specter is floating
         VERB

above this _____! Now do you believe in _____?
                NOUN   PLURAL NOUN

MAD LIBS® is fun to play with friends, but you can also play it by yourself! To begin with, DO NOT look at the story on the page below. Fill in the blanks on this page with the words called for. Then, using the words you have selected, fill in the blank spaces in the story.

Now you've created your own hilarious MAD LIBS® game!

A GHOSTLY FAIRY TALE

NOUN _____

ADJECTIVE _____

VERB ENDING IN "ING" _____

PART OF THE BODY (PLURAL) _____

NOUN _____

VERB ENDING IN "ING" _____

NOUN _____

VERB _____

SOMETHING ALIVE _____

NOUN _____

VERB (PAST TENSE) _____

A SOUND _____

VERB _____

ADJECTIVE _____

ARTICLE OF CLOTHING _____

PART OF THE BODY _____

NOUN _____

ADVERB _____

MAD LIBS®

A GHOSTLY FAIRY TALE

Once upon a/an _____ , a/an _____ knight was protecting
　　　　　　　　　NOUN　　　　　　　　　ADJECTIVE

a castle when, suddenly, the ghost of a fire-_____
　　　　　　　　　　　　　　　　　　　　　　　VERB ENDING IN "ING"

dragon appeared! The knight's _____ shook as
　　　　　　　　　　　　　　　PART OF THE BODY (PLURAL)

he pulled out his sharp _____ and declared, "Stay back,
　　　　　　　　　　　　　NOUN

ghostly dragon! I am Sir William of _____-ham,
　　　　　　　　　　　　　　　　　VERB ENDING IN "ING"

brave knight of the Round _____! You can't _____
　　　　　　　　　　　　　NOUN　　　　　　　　　　VERB

me!" But then, the fire-breathing _____ shot a hot
　　　　　　　　　　　　　　　　SOMETHING ALIVE

_____ at the knight! Fortunately, the knight
　　　　NOUN

_____ under the fireball, which smashed into the castle
　VERB (PAST TENSE)

wall behind him, making a huge _____! When the smoke
　　　　　　　　　　　　　　　A SOUND

cleared, the knight said, "And the reason you can't _____ me
　　　　　　　　　　　　　　　　　　　　　　　VERB

is because I am already _____." The knight pulled off his
　　　　　　　　　　　ADJECTIVE

metal _____ and revealed . . . he was a ghost, too!
　　　ARTICLE OF CLOTHING

Frustrated, the ghost dragon slapped its _____ on the
　　　　　　　　　　　　　　　　　　PART OF THE BODY

ground and soared away under the light of the full _____.
　　　　　　　　　　　　　　　　　　　　　　　NOUN

And the people of the kingdom lived _____ ever after.
　　　　　　　　　　　　　　　　　ADVERB

MAD LIBS® is fun to play with friends, but you can also play it by yourself! To begin with, DO NOT look at the story on the page below. Fill in the blanks on this page with the words called for. Then, using the words you have selected, fill in the blank spaces in the story.

Now you've created your own hilarious MAD LIBS® game!

GHOST STEW RECIPE

VERB _____

SOMETHING ALIVE (PLURAL) _____

VERB _____

ADJECTIVE _____

NOUN _____

NUMBER _____

SOMETHING ALIVE _____

NOUN _____

NOUN _____

NUMBER _____

VERB _____

ANIMAL _____

TYPE OF LIQUID _____

A PLACE _____

TYPE OF FOOD _____

ADJECTIVE _____

TYPE OF CONTAINER _____

NUMBER _____

MAD LIBS®

GHOST STEW RECIPE

Contrary to what some people _____, ghosts do not eat
<u>VERB</u>

_____. They _____ _____
SOMETHING ALIVE (PLURAL)   VERB   ADJECTIVE

food just like you and me! So, if you find yourself with a phantom

_____ at the dinner table, here's a recipe for a ghost stew that
NOUN

ghosts won't say "Boo" to:

1. Pour _____ cans of _____ broth into a large
    NUMBER   SOMETHING ALIVE

   _____ and heat on low.
   NOUN

2. Peel 1 _____ and simmer in the broth for _____
    NOUN   NUMBER

   hours.

3. _____ 3 pounds of _____ -flavored
    VERB   ANIMAL

   tofu into cubes and add them to the broth.

4. Add in 19 cups of _____ from (the) _____.
    TYPE OF LIQUID   A PLACE

5. Add 1 brown _____ to the broth and stir until it is
    TYPE OF FOOD

   _____.
   ADJECTIVE

6. Serve in a/an _____. Makes enough for
    TYPE OF CONTAINER

   _____ ghosts.
   NUMBER

MAD LIBS® is fun to play with friends, but you can also play it by yourself! To begin with, DO NOT look at the story on the page below. Fill in the blanks on this page with the words called for. Then, using the words you have selected, fill in the blank spaces in the story.

Now you've created your own hilarious MAD LIBS® game!

CAPTAIN FOOLHARDY'S CURSED TREASURE

ADJECTIVE _____

A PLACE _____

NOUN _____

VEHICLE _____

PLURAL NOUN _____

TYPE OF FOOD _____

TYPE OF LIQUID _____

NUMBER _____

PERSON YOU KNOW _____

VERB (PAST TENSE) _____

TYPE OF CONTAINER _____

NOUN _____

PLURAL NOUN _____

VERB _____

VERB (PAST TENSE) _____

OCCUPATION _____

NOUN _____

ADJECTIVE _____

MAD LIBS
CAPTAIN FOOLHARDY'S
CURSED TREASURE

A long time ago, a/an _____ pirate named Captain Foolhardy

ADJECTIVE

hid his treasure on the shores of a tropical _____ in the

A PLACE

middle of the ocean. But while the pirates were on the island, a deadly

_____ sank their _____, trapping the captain and

NOUN　　　　　　　　　VEHICLE

his crew of _____ without any _____ or

PLURAL NOUN　　　　　　　　TYPE OF FOOD

_____. _____ years later, an explorer named

TYPE OF LIQUID　　　NUMBER

_____ the Great _____ on that island

PERSON YOU KNOW　　　　VERB (PAST TENSE)

and discovered the captain's cursed _____ of treasure.

TYPE OF CONTAINER

When the explorer pried open the treasure chest, the ghost of Captain

_____-hardy flew out and said, "Shiver me _____!

NOUN　　　　　　　　　　　　　　　　　PLURAL NOUN

Who be trying to _____ me bounty?" The explorer

VERB

_____ backward in the sand at the sight of the menacing

VERB (PAST TENSE)

_____ and then begged to be allowed to sail home. In exchange

OCCUPATION

for his _____, the explorer promised to never tell anyone about

NOUN

the treasure. But the ghost of the captain only replied: " _____

ADJECTIVE

men tell no tales!" And the explorer was never heard from again.